# HOW I BECAME A BIG MONEY SPEAKER

## ...AND HOW YOU CAN TOO!

*The 10 Mistakes to Avoid*

*When Adding Public Speaking to Your Current Business!*

**JAMES MALINCHAK**

THE BIG MONEY SPEAKER  *www.BigMoneySpeaker.com*

Glazer-Kennedy
publishing

*Imprint of Morgan James Publishing*
NEW YORK

# HOW I BECAME A BIG MONEY SPEAKER

## ...AND HOW YOU CAN TOO!

### by James Malinchak

Copyright © 2010 James Malinchak International, Inc.
All rights reserved.

ISBN 978-0-98237-933-2 (paperback)
Library of Congress Control Number: 2009936849

**Published by:**

Glazer-Kennedy
publishing

*an imprint of*
Morgan James Publishing, LLC
1225 Franklin Ave. Ste 325
Garden City, NY 11530-1693
Toll Free 800-485-4943
www.MorganJamesPublishing.com

Cover/Interior Design by:
Rachel Lopez
rachel@r2cdesign.com

In an effort to support local communities, raise awareness and funds, Morgan James Publishing donates one percent of all book sales for the life of each book to Habitat for Humanity.
Get involved today, visit
**www.HelpHabitatForHumanity.org.**

# DISCLAIMER

*The purpose of this book* is to inform and entertain. The author or publisher does not guarantee or promise that anyone following the techniques, suggestions, tips, ideas, examples, illustrations or strategies, will become successful or achieve any financial gain. The author and publisher shall have neither liability nor responsibility to anyone with respect to any loss or damage caused, or alleged to be caused, directly or indirectly by the information contained in this book and these writings.

# TABLE OF CONTENTS

# Dan Kennedy & Bill Glazer Select James Malinchak As Their 2008-2009 Marketer of the Year!

*"I want to congratulate James for winning the very prestigious (GKIC) Marketer of the Year Award...He's a very smart information marketer!"*

-DAN KENNEDY, **Marketing Guru**

*"The thing I like about James Malinchak is, not only is he a great coach for teaching people how to get into the speaking business, but James recently won our (GKIC) Marketer of the Year Award. And the reason he won that is not only because he can be a great speaking coach. But he's so well-rounded that he can help and coach entrepreneurs in any walk-of-life of how to really grow their businesses. So he's fully dimensional and if you seek him out and work with him, you've made a great choice!"*

-BILL GLAZER, **President Glazer-Kennedy Insider's Circle**

# WHAT TOP ACHIEVERS ARE SAYING ABOUT JAMES MALINCHAK...

## *"Made Over $40,000.00!*

*I was learning from the best, Donald Trump, who is a brilliant marketer! But do you know what? You can learn from someone even better, James Malinchak! He is so good and has taught me so much! I have been learning from James for about 2 ½ years now and this weekend alone, <u>I just made over $40,000.</u> <u>So learn from James. He knows what he's doing.</u> <u>He's the BEST!</u>"*

-KRISTI FRANK, **Top Competitor Season #1 of Donald Trump's The Apprentice**

# *"James Malinchak's Coaching for Me Has Been Incredibly Helpful!"*

*"James Malinchak's coaching for me on how to sell more product and enroll more people in my trainings from the platform has been incredibly helpful in terms of increasing our revenues, sharing our materials with more people and touching more lives! So I am deeply grateful for his incredible wisdom about it, his ability to impart that wisdom so that I was actually able to incorporate it. I have been the one who was kind of reluctant to sell because I just saw myself as a person changing the world and James helped me realize I could really change the world even more by getting more people to take my materials home with them. If you're thinking about taking James' programs or thinking about buying his audio programs or his video programs that will help you sell more so that you can have more income and more impact I really strongly encourage you to do that!"*

-Jack Canfield, **Author of the best-selling book,** *The Success Principles* **& his latest book,** *Keys to Living the Law of Attraction* **Co-creator of the #1 best-selling book series** *Chicken Soup for the Soul* **& Featured Expert in the Block-Buster Movie,** *The Secret*

## *"One of the Best in the World!"*

*"James Malinchak is one of the best speakers, trainers, teachers of coaching and speaking in the world today. You can learn more from a seminar with James, from getting involved in James's in his platinum club circle than you can all by yourself working for years and years and years. So if you want to shorten your learning curve, dramatically increase your income and your results and your success with speaking, you've got to get involved with James!"*

-BRIAN TRACY, **Top selling author of over 45 books, Has Addressed more than 4,000,000 people in 4,000 talks and seminars throughout the US, Canada and 40 other countries worldwide**

## *"Sold More Than $40,000!"*

*"I've been speaking professionally for more than 15 years. I have spoken everywhere from Beijing to Budapest and I sold nothing, nothing before I learned how to sell from the platform of James Malinchak. Since I've taken his personal training, I've sold more than $40,000.00 worth of product and services from the platform. Thank you so much James, you've made a big difference in my life."*

-DAN JANAL, **President PRLeads**

## *"6-Figures In A Month!"*

*"I just finished my one day with James at his home in Las Vegas. We had such a great time. I'm the founder of the Grief Coach Academy and James has helped me so much. When I started coaching with him, my goal was to make six figures a year. <u>I just recently did six figures in a month.</u> And now with my one day with him, I can easily see how it's going to be possible to make seven figures. No problem, thanks to James's excellent coaching."*

-Aurora Winter **(Los Angeles, CA)**

## *"I Sold Almost $200,000 Worth of Products From a Single Teleseminar In Less Than 72-hours. Thank You James!"*

*"I am SO EXCITED to tell you that I spent a day with James at his house and I learned SO MUCH and I implemented it all immediately. I am proud to report that just a few weeks later, really just 30-days, I sold almost $200,000 worth of products from a single teleseminar in less than 72-hours. Thank you James!"*

-Kendall Summerhawk, **The Money, Marketing & Soul Coach for Women**

# "*Worth Millions & Millions of Dollars!*"

"*I'm always a little skeptical when I meet an expert, because it seems like everybody's an expert. Three years ago, getting to know James, I had something really, really powerful happen. James became my go to person. I am a speaker, I do a lot of speaking and when I get asked to speak somewhere, James is the first person I contact. Because I want for me to see my strategy, my tips, even if I'm going to go to an event, I want to know everything that can maximize my profit and give me the best returns both from client base and money when I'm on stage. So do yourself a huge favor, make James your go to person. He's got it going on and you want to know what's in his head, because it's worth millions and millions of dollars in your pocket.*"

-MELANIE BENSON STRICK, **the Entrepreneur**

**Success Coach (Sherman Oaks, CA)**

**& Glazer-Kennedy Insider's Circle Member**

# "I've been involved in speaking for 40+ years, I've seen them all...There's no one better than James Malinchak!"

"I just listen to James Malinchak make a presentation to a group and he absolutely blew the group away. I've been doing this for about forty years now; consulting with companies, corporations and associations. Working with individuals, helping them make their businesses stronger, better and more profitable. I've been involved in speaking for 40+ years, I've seen them all. When it come to training people how to speak, how to make presentations, effective presentations; presentations that will put money in your pocket, there's no one better than James Malinchak. He's my coach, he's the one I depend on!"

-MARTIN HOWEY, **Top Line Business Solutions**

**(Consultant for 40+ Years)**

# "As an Event Promoter...There Is Only One Person I Send Them to and That's Mr. James Malinchak!"

"As an event promoter and also a person that owns a marketing company that works with many different speakers, I've had the experience where I've worked with people from motivation to health and fitness to the real estate industry behind the scenes. _And when I need to teach them how to learn to speak from a stage and sell to make money and make a presentation that I know gets results, there is only one person I send them to and that's Mr. James Malinchak._ If you want to learn to be an affective speaker, there's a lot of resources you can to, but if you want to learn how to be effective and make money, then there's only one resource you need. It's worth your time to make an investment in not only your business and yourself with Mr. James Malinchak and it will make the biggest difference and you will be happy you did it. So just do it!"

-KENDRA CECEITA, Beverly, MA

## *"Absolutely PHOENOMINAL!"*

*"I just finished James Malinchak's seminar and it's absolutely PHOENOMINAL! If you are in the business of becoming a speaker or if you are looking to become a speaker, or if you're putting on a seminar, then I can't even begin to tell you how crazy you would be not to come to James' Boot Camp. It has been a real privilege and a real honor to be here and I have learned a TON and I can't wait to get more involved with James!"*

-RON SEAVER, **President, National Sports Forum**

**& Glazer-Kennedy Insider's Circle Member**

# "There's Stuff Here That James Revealed That I've Never, Ever Heard Any Other Speaker or Seen Revealed at Any Other Boot Camp!"

"I had the privilege of being here at the Millionaire Speaker boot camp and it was just absolutely fabulous. There's stuff here that James revealed that I've never, ever heard any other speaker or seen revealed at any other boot camp. <u>So if you want to learn how to make big money and how to influence your audience, James is the guy that I recommend....If you want to learn how to make big money as a speaker and influence people, James is your guy.</u> So just take my word and just do it."

-MARLENE GREEN, President Millionaire Blueprints™ Magazine (N.Y./N.J.) and Chapter Director of Glazer Kennedy Insider Circle™ Manhattan, NY

# *"Even NBA World Champion Coach Says James Is the Best!"*

*"Hey I'm Doc Rivers. I'm the Head Coach of the Boston Celtics, World Champs. Listen, obviously, for our run, we needed inspiration. If you need it, this is your man. James is the best. I should have used you more before the championship. But I'm serious, absolutely terrific, I've read his book and it's great. Great stuff. It will help you!"*

-DOC RIVERS, **Head Coach of**

**The World Champion Boston Celtics**

# An Apology To You Ahead Of Time...

*I need to apologize,* ahead of time, as I know that I may seem to come across as a bit aggressive in what you're about to read. I do it for one reason, and one reason only:

*I don't want you to make the same mistakes I did!*

I truly want you to be as successful as you desire to be and believe, without a doubt, that what you're about to read will change your life.

You don't need to agree with what I'm about to share. But I would like ask for you to have an open mind. Simply have an open mind to seriously consider adopting my way of thinking about the speaking industry. I know from my experience that what I'm about to share with you in this short book will tremendously help you.

Before Reading This Short Book, I Must Offer You A...

# WARNING:

- If you are expecting me to sugar-coat the realities of the speaking industry…STOP READING!

- If you don't like someone who is direct, straight-forward, and to the point…STOP READING!

- If you are expecting to hear the same old BS stuff you've heard others repeat year after year in the speaking industry…STOP READING!

One thing I can promise you is that I will NOT BS you and give you "fluff!" I can't stand when people in the speaking industry do that to entrepreneurs like us.

Why? Because that's what many in the speaking industry did to me back when I was broke, "spinning my wheels," and not booking any talks or making any money as a speaker. My style is direct, straight-forward and I don't pull punches. My sole focus is to help you and give you simple ideas that will instantly save and possibly make you big money! And, I think you'll appreciate the fact that I'm direct and to-the-point! I think you and I are probably a lot alike!

I think you want someone who is willing to cut through the crap and just tell you what you <u>NEED</u> to know to stop wasting money and to make a big money! Sometimes in life we need someone to be direct and tell us something that we may not like to hear, but that we <u>NEED</u> to hear!

I often compare this to taking a terrible dose of cough syrup. You may not like the taste when it's going down, but you know that once it's digested, your aches and pains will disappear and you will be better.

It's the same for what I'm about to share with you! You may not like the taste, but I guarantee that you'll be 100% better after this "speaking cough syrup" gets digested. Because I truly care about helping you save and make more money, I'm about to give you the BEST medicine you could ever have for your speaking business!

Are you ready?…Hope so…because this information is priceless and will save, and can make, you BIG MONEY!

Thank you for taking the time to read this short and simple book!

To your wealth,

James Malinchak

**www.BigMoneySpeaker.com**
**www.MillionaireSpeakerSecrets.com**

# INTRODUCTION

*Let's get started with* a couple of questions.

*Question #1:*

Are you ready to make an <u>extra</u> $100,000, $250,000, $500,000 or even $1,000,000 for talking about stuff you already know?

*Question #2:*

Are you ready to attract more clients in the next 90 days or less than you got all last year?

*Question #3:*

Are you ready to get paid big checks for talking about stuff you already know that you would talk about anyway?

If you answered yes to any of these questions, then I have good news for you. You're in the right place, at the right time and this is the right message for you.

My name is James Malinchak and I am here to tell you that you have been missing out on one of the greatest, most overlooked, most untapped, most lucrative business niches…public speaking. And I wrote this short and simple book to help you to potentially stop losing out on hundreds of thousands (maybe even millions) of dollars you don't even realize you are losing out on and to inform you of why you should add public speaking as one of your income streams.

Let me ask you a question. Do you have a story or a message of hope, motivation, personal success or business achievement you believe can help other people? If you answered yes, then public speaking is a niche that you could add to your current business that can literally help you double, even triple your current income.

Two important points before we get started.

1.  First, you will quickly learn that I don't BS people. I'm a straight-shooter-type of person and I tell it like it is. I can't stand when people in the speaking industry BS people who are thinking about possibly adding public speaking to their current business. Why? Because that's what many in the speaking industry did to me back when I was broke, "spinning my wheels," and not booking any talks

or making any money in public speaking. My style is direct, straight-forward and I don't pull punches. I know this information will help you because I have been there where you are trying to figure out how to really make big money from public speaking. <u>I am just like you!</u>

I know that I may seem to come across as a bit aggressive in what you're about to read. I do it for one reason, and one reason only. Because I truly want you to be as successful as you desire to be and believe, without a doubt, that what you're about to read will change your life. I know from my experience that what I'm about to share with you will tremendously help you.

2. Secondly, I can't possibly teach you everything you need to know about making big money in public speaking in this short, little book. I do an entire four-day intense live

Big Money Speaking Success Boot Camp (**www.BigMoneySpeaker.com** and **www.Millionaire SpeakerSecrets.com**) where we really dive into several aspects of How to Make Big Money Speaking and how it's possible to double, even triple, your income. The Boot Camps begin at 8:00 AM and end around 8:00 PM each night and it is the BEST training there is for the speaking business...period! Nothing even comes close to the details I share with you in my trainings! (Just look at the numerous testimonials from people just like you and the high-profile celebrity speakers, authors, trainers, coaches, consultants, Internet marketers and info-preneurs who have been to my training events.)

So there's no possible way I could cram all of the information into a book or the book would literally be over 1,000 pages. What I will do in this short book is to provide you with great information that will allow you to see the potential for what's possible for you. Are you ready? I hope so because this information is priceless and can save, and make, you a ton of money!

In this short book, I'm going to share with you some simple ideas cover just two parts that will give you insight into how I went from not knowing anything to making big money with public speaking and insight into what to avoid so you don't encounter some of the pitfalls I faced when adding public speaking to my business.

Basically, this book is divided into two short parts:

- **<u>Part #1:</u>** How I Got Started Making Big Money As a Public Speaker...And It Was All By Accident!
- **<u>Part #2:</u>** The 10 Mistakes to Avoid When Adding Public Speaking to Your Current Business!

I said this book was short and it's intended to give you a better idea and understanding of the mistakes to avoid that can cause

So, let's get started...

# PART ONE

*How I Got Started
Making Big Money
As a Public Speaker
...And It Was
All By Accident!*

# CHAPTER 1

# How I Got Started Making Big Money As a Public Speaker

## ...And It Was All By Accident!

S o who am I and why should you listen to me?

That's a fair question and one that I would ask, too, because as I learned from one of my Platinum Coaching members Jonathan Sprinkles, a speaker who has attended 22 of my live Big Money Speaking Success Boot Camp trainings (**www.BigMoneySpeaker.com** and **www.MillionaireSpeakerSecrets.com**), *"no one will ever hear you until they know you!"*

(By the way, Jonathan has made a TON of money as a public speaker and there is a direct correlation between him being a constant Boot Camp attendee and much of his financial success).

First of all, please understand that I am nothing special with no special talents or skills and

I certainly wasn't born into speaking success and wealth!

I was raised in a small steel-mill town in Western Pennsylvania that you've probably never heard of called Monessen. Although my Mom and Dad were kind-hearted, hard-working people who supported my sisters, brother and me, growing up we didn't have much in terms of financial resources. My Mom was a housewife taking care of us while my Dad busted his butt working hard in the local steel-mill making $29,000 a year.

Like many young teenagers, I had big dreams, one of which was to land a college basketball scholarship. However, I began listening to certain negative-thinking people who told me that it couldn't be done because of what they said...I wasn't good enough...or because I wasn't smart enough...or because I lived in a small steel-mill town. (Have you ever been told that you couldn't do something?)

I went through a period where I continuously doubted myself and stopped believing that I could achieve my dream of playing college basketball. This self-doubt continued for a few years until a high school teacher named Mrs. Monaghan said something to me that changed my life. She said,

*"James Malinchak, it's ridiculous for you to listen to anyone who is telling you that you can't achieve your dream because IF YOU CAN DREAM IT, THEN YOU CAN DO IT!"*

That ONE statement and that ONE person believing in me was the TURNING POINT in my life that led me to, not only achieving my dream of landing a full-basketball scholarship to the University of Cincinnati, but also led me throughout my life achieving many more BIG dreams, including creating a hugely successful speaking career and achieving financial freedom by age 34 where I could do what I want, when I want, where I want, while never having to ever worry about paying the bills or having to live within a budget.

Have you ever had one person in your life who has given you the permission to create a turning point for yourself? Maybe it was a teacher...maybe it was a parent...maybe it was a friend...maybe it was mentor or a coach...or, maybe it will even be me in this book, which if it is, then I am truly honored and thankful!

Out of high school, I accepted that basketball scholarship to the University of Cincinnati before transferring when my coach got fired. I then played at and graduated from the University of Hawaii at Hilo, before moving to Los Angeles, where I started my career as a stockbroker with a major Wall Street Investment Firm. I did pretty well as a stockbroker and, because of that, I got asked to give a talk to some of the younger brokers.

## So, Just How Did I Get Started Making Big Money with Public Speaking?

First, I never planned on being a speaker. I didn't wake up one day and say, "I want to be a speaker."

I didn't know ANYTHING about speaking, the industry or how to make money. I mean literally NOTHING, which is good news for you because if I could go from not knowing anything about the speaking business to making millions of dollars, then you can as well. You just need to know the right recipe with the right ingredients.

It all began several years ago when I was working as a stockbroker I developed a dream. I had the dream, vision and desire to help college students who were just like me... just an average everyday "c" student. I was what my friend Professor Joe Martin calls a "see your way through college" type of student.

While in college, I was told by numerous people that I couldn't land my "dream-job" (which was to be a stockbroker with a major Wall Street Investment Firm) because I didn't have great grades or because I wasn't the President of certain student organizations on campus. And, I believed what I was being told.

Finally, as my senior year was in full swing, I quickly realized the "real world" was fast approaching and that soon mom and dad wouldn't be there to cover my bills. It was time for me to start taking responsibility for myself... and, oh, yah...my bills that would start coming due when I got out of college.

Basically, out of fear, I decided I needed to stop listening to all those people who were telling me I couldn't land my dream job and it was time to start doing something about it. Despite hearing all the reasons why I couldn't do it, I decided I would find a way to overcome the fact my grades weren't the best and that I WOULD land my dream-job.

To make a long story short, because of determination and because of the fact I learned how to package, market and sell myself to employers, I was able to land three different job offers, three months prior to graduation, in the city I wanted to live in working for the company for whom I wanted to work.

About a month prior to actually graduating from college, it finally hit me. There needs to be a book like this to help students who are just like me; average, everyday 'c' students who have the desire to land a particular job but believe they can't do it because they may not have the best grades.

So, I immediately decided to write a book to help students. My dream was born!

It took me about three years to finish the book because I knew absolutely nothing about how to write a book. I decided to self-publish the book because not one publisher took me seriously. Fortunately, I came across a book that taught me step-by-step how to self-publish my book.

I did it! I self-published my book and felt awesome when I received my 1,000 copies. Do you remember that awesome feeling when you finally finished your first book?

I remember like it was yesterday.

However, I also remember the terrible, sickening feeling that started to develop after about a week of getting my 1,000 copies of the book. Do you know what feeling I'm talking about? The feeling of: *It's great that I have my book, but I'm still out the thousands of dollars it cost me to publish the book!* All of a sudden, the awesome feeling was nowhere to be found as reality set in as the bills were coming due for the production of the book.

I realized, although it was great to turn my dream, vision and desire to help college students into a book, I was still broke and still had these book production bills coming due. I needed to do something and I needed to do it fast!

Out of desperation, I picked up the telephone book and began searching for any and all colleges within a 50-mile radius. I called professors at these schools and asked if I could speak for their classes. My plan was to speak for free and try to sell copies of my book. And, it worked.

I remember my very first talk was for about 30 students for a professor's class. I sold 10 books at $10 each and made a $100. I remember thinking this was great! I only needed to do this another 30+ times and I would be able to pay all of the book production bills. I did about 70-80 talks for free before I ever knew you could get paid to speak.

Although at that moment, it seemed like a good idea to be doing all of these talks, I soon realized it took a lot of time, energy and effort. I needed to do something different as it was becoming a lot of work trying to get professors on the phone, schedule a day and time to speak, and drive all over the state simply to make $100.

I needed help. I needed an easier way.

Then, one day during a casual conversation with a professor, he asked if I knew that schools have certain coordinators who bring speakers to their campuses and even pay them and pay them well. I told him that I had no idea.

There it was…the help I needed…the easier way I had hoped existed was knocking right on my front door.

And since that day, I never looked back and never struggled again. From that day, I've been a public speaker for corporations, associations, entrepreneur groups, community organizations, colleges, universities, youth groups and have hosted numerous of my own public seminars.

And, now…

I have done over 2,200 presentations for entrepreneur groups, corporations, community groups, universities, colleges, and even large youth-type events. Yet, you probably have never heard of me, which goes to prove you don't need to be a famous speaker to be a successful and wealthy speaker!

I have walked out of events with $30,000, $100,000 and even $1,000,000. I hear people say all of the time, *"Nobody can make money that kind of money from public speaking!"* And I often think to myself how sad it is for these people to believe this. They just don't know how to do it and because they don't know how to do it, they use the excuse that it can't possibly be done. They are really selling themselves short of what's possible and are leaving a TON of money on the table because I know how to do it and several entrepreneurs I've taught in my live Boot Camps now know how to do it, too...and are doing it!

I've been paid to deliver presentations all over the United States, including vacation destinations like Hawaii, Las Vegas, Orlando, Palm Springs and have also traveled to the Bahamas, Bermuda, Canada, and Mexico to speak.

I've even been on programs with celebrities such as: basketball superstar Michael Jordan, former world heavyweight boxing champion George Foreman, the inspiration behind the Tri-Star blockbuster movie *RUDY*– Danielle "Rudy" Ruettiger, *Chicken Soup for the Soul®* Co-Creators, Jack Canfield and Mark Victor Hansen and various contestants from Donald Trump's blockbuster TV show, *The Apprentice*.

I'm a featured expert in the blockbuster movie PASS IT ON with such top speakers as Brian Tracy, Les Brown, John Assaraf, Rev. Michael Beckwith, Mark Victor Hansen and others. I've coached and trained thousands of wonderful people just like you (whether you're just starting or are experienced) and have helped many of the top high-profile celebrity speakers, authors, trainers, coaches, consultants, Internet marketers and info-preneurs who have been to my training events. And, I've even coached TV personalities on how to turn their story into a lucrative speaking career.

<u>I didn't tell you about my background to impress you. I told you about it because I always remember that I grew-up in a small steel mill town and knew absolutely nothing about public speaking when I started. What this means to you is if I can go from where I was to having all this success as a public speaker, so can you!</u>

# Started Getting Asked to Teach Others How to Speak and Make Big Money!

To bring the story full-circle...

Because of what I've been blessed to accomplish with public speaking, others found out about me through casual conversation (because I never told anyone my secrets for how I was pulling down some serious money) and began inviting me to speak to their groups at their events.

I've been invited to speak at numerous live events and on numerous tele-seminars by major niched marketing gurus like:

| | |
|---|---|
| Dan Kennedy | Mark Victor Hansen |
| Matt Bacak | Bill Glazer |
| Alexandria Brown | Paul Hartunian |
| Jack Canfield | Milana Leshinsky |
| Kendall Summerhawk | Mari Smith |
| John Childers | Martin Howey |
| Adam Urbanski | Tom Antion |
| Raleigh Pinskey | Dottie Walters |
| Debbie Allen | Dan Janal |
| Susan Levin | Bill & Steve Harrison |
| Ed O'Keefe | And numerous others! |

# IMPORTANT TO NOTE:

## *I Don't Have Any Advanced Degrees or Any Speaker Industry Designations*

I need to tell you something that is VERY important.

First, I don't have any-type of advanced academic degrees whatsoever, meaning I don't have a Masters Degree nor do I have a Ph.D.

Secondly, I don't have any-type of speaker designations from any speaker associations whatsoever and I've never entered (and for sure have never won) any kind of speaking competition. I did get voted college speaker of the year twice, but that wasn't because of me. That was because of the program I created that was changing students lives. Honestly, I believe that I am only an average speaker.

Why this is important to you is that <u>I am just like you and I am living proof that you don't need advanced academic degrees and you don't need speaker certifications in order to make big money with public speaking.</u>

I have a little saying that I'm constantly preaching to speakers who attend my live Big Money Speaking Success Boot Camp and who are in my Millionaire Speaker Wealth Attraction Platinum Coaching Program. And, I want you to really get this:

*"Don't fill your ego, fill your bank account!"*

While other people in public speaking are pursuing completing paperwork so they can get those speaker certifications or to enter public speaking competitions, <u>I want you to focus on making money with public speaking!</u>

Don't waste your time and energy worrying about winning competitions or getting designations.

I want you to have only one designation, which is an

**MBA:**

**M: MASSIVE**

**B: BANK**

**A: ACCOUNT**

If I gave you a choice between having a speaking ribbon, trophy or certification or having a Massive Bank Account so you can have more than enough money to do what you want, when you want, where you want, which would you choose? If you didn't choose the Massive Bank Account, then please stop reading because that is exactly what I show speakers in my coaching programs, live boot camps, and home study courses how to rapidly create for themselves! So, if that bothers you, then this isn't the right book for you.

## SPEAKING IS AS SIMPLE AS FOLLOWING A RECIPE?

That's right!

I think creating a successful, lucrative public speaking business is not difficult. If you haven't done so yet, it's not your fault. You just haven't been taught the <u>right</u> recipe!

Again, please understand that I'm nothing special. What I've done is to create the RIGHT step-by-step, easy-to-follow RECIPE for making big money as a highly paid public speaker. There's NO guess-work involved as I've done ALL the work for you. My RECIPE has worked for me over and over and it's worked for numerous entrepreneurs JUST LIKE YOU over and over...and it can work for YOU over and over! Simply follow my proven, time-tested, step-by-step RECIPE!

A Recipe?!?!

Yes! Let me explain.

I've never baked a cake. However, I know that if you simply handed me the right RECIPE on an index card that told me which ingredients to get at the store, which ingredient to mix in the bowl first, which to mix second, which to mix third, and so on, which temperature to set the oven on, and how long to bake the cake in the oven, then I know that I could bake the cake...if I simply follow the proven, time-tested RECIPE.

It's exactly the same for making big money with public speaking. Just as there is a recipe for baking a cake, I have created a proven, time-tested RECIPE for making big money with public speaking. This recipe was first created for me to follow, which I have for the past 14 years with tremendous success. It's the same recipe I've shared with entrepreneurs just like you in my live Boot Camps, Coaching Groups and Home Study Courses (**www.BigMoneySpeaker.com**)

## A Big Secret Shared With Me From a Rich Mentor

I remember back when I first began public speaking like it was yesterday. I can't even begin to tell you how discouraged I became.

There were SO many times when I thought about "throwing in the towel" and walking away from pursuing my dream of getting paid to speak and share my message. I seemed to be just "spinning my wheels" and often felt like a complete failure!

At one point, I lived in a tiny apartment on Brand Boulevard in Glendale, California that was so bad, there were actually steel bars on the windows to make sure nobody would break in. I even slept every night with baseball bat just in case there was a break-in while I was sleeping (I'm not kidding).

Financially, it was getting tougher and tougher! Bills were coming in that I just couldn't cover.

I tried everything to make more money speaking, but NOTHING seemed to work. I had no idea what to do! I was about to fall flat on my face and give-up, when one day...

## *A Turning Point...*

I was talking on the phone with a friend, who's very successful in business and a multimillionaire. While we were catching-up, I asked him why most of his businesses were successful.

I figured he would say something about his extensive business knowledge or 35+ years of experience. But his answer shocked me...and became the "KEY" that was the "turning point" for my entire speaking career!

He said,

*"The reason is simple, and is what I actually consider to be the key for anyone to succeed in ANY industry, even the speaking industry, James! The reason is because*

*I don't study and learn from top experts in my industry,
like so many others do who fail in my industry.
I study and learn from the world's <u>top MARKETERS!</u>"*

"What?  I'm not sure I follow you," I replied.
He continued,

*"Nobody in ANY business could ever be successful if they
don't know how to correctly market their products or
services and get people to buy them. Just because someone
is a top expert in your industry, doesn't mean they know
how to market. So, why would I want to spend my time
and possibly waste my money trying to study and learn
from them?  I'd rather just go right out and study and
learn from the world's top MARKETERS because they
know how to do one thing better than anyone, <u>MAKE
MONEY FROM MARKETING!</u>"*

# IMMEDIATELY, A LIGHT BULB WENT OFF IN MY HEAD!

I knew my wealthy, successful cousin wouldn't have said
that if he didn't mean it 100%. What if I did the same!?!
What if I studied and learned from the world's top
marketers and took what I learned and simply applied it

to the speaking industry!?! Surely, it would work because principles are principles!

So, that's what I began doing, and let me tell you, focusing on that one "shift in my thinking" <u>INSTANTLY</u> changed my career. I mean, <u>INSTANTLY!</u>

I went from where I was, "spinning my wheels" beginning as speaker, feeling like a complete failure, ready to give-up and quit, to booking over 100 paid talks within 24-months and making hundreds of thousands of dollars.

See, I know what you're probably going through because I've been there. And, I understand how frustrating it can be to know that YOU have the potential to make big money, but for some unexplained reason it just doesn't happen!

Don't let this bring you down, because I've been there many times in the past. Although it can be frustrating at times, here's some good news.

YOU can achieve anything you desire as a speaker. You can impact and positively change lives while making big money with public speaking.

I KNOW YOU CAN DO IT!

Because, I truly believe that if I did it and continue doing it every year, then anyone can! <u>I'm nothing special!</u> I just got sick and tired of struggling and being broke!

## *Now, I'm On A Personal Mission!*

So, why did I write this short and simple book? My sole purpose for writing it is to help you and to hopefully give you what my cousin gave to me:

*I want to inspire you to immediately
"<u>shift your thinking</u>" about public speaking.*

If I can share with you some ideas that will help you to avoid losing the large amounts of money I've lost, or if I can help you make a lot more money, then my purpose will be fulfilled.

And, boy did I lose money. I remember blowing about $10,000 by doing one thing that I heard a "*a top expert in the speaking industry*" tell a group of us entrepreneurs to do! I'm not kidding!

I did exactly what he said to do, spent $10,000 and didn't even get one call! Not one call!

See, if I could go from those dismal beginnings when I started my speaking career, to having the kind of success that I'm now blessed to experience, then I know YOU can achieve any of your public speaking dreams, too!

Over the years, many talented entrepreneurs have approached me when they found out the kind of money

I make each year <u>without winning any kind of speaking industry awards,</u> <u>having a New York Times best-selling book, or being a famous.</u>

And, to be honest, I really don't even think I'm that great of a speaker. Personally, I don't think you need to be a great speaker to make a ton of money! And, it annoys me when people in the speaking industry program you to believe that.

It doesn't matter if you're a great public speaker or not. You can achieve all of your public speaking goals and can make a big money.

How do I know that the short and simple tips in this book can help you?

Because, these are the <u>exact</u> marketing tips that I used to transform myself when I was living back in that tiny apartment in Glendale, California, "spinning my wheels," trying to figure out how to pay my overdue bills as I was just about to quit in public speaking.

And, these are the <u>exact</u> marketing tips that numerous entrepreneurs who've attended my Big Money Speaking Success Boot Camps (**www.BigMoneySpeaker.com** and **www.MillionaireSpeakerSecrets.com**) were making prior to me <u>shifting their thinking!</u>

Once they did shift their thinking, their incomes began exploding. For example, here's what just a few have said after "making the shift"...

> *"I stopped trying to count the dollars when I got to $250,000 in extra product sales that I made from James' techniques. My whole career was changed! James has taught me how to think like a <u>MARKETER</u>, not a speaker!"*
>
> -Jonathan Sprinkles **(Houston, TX)**

> *"I've made at least $100,000 from following James' strategies!"*
>
> -Professor Joe Martin **(Tallahassee, FL)**

Now, I'm on a personal mission! I want to touch the lives and impact the bank accounts of as many entrepreneurs around the world as possible...including your life and your bank account!

So, I'd like to ask for your help. If, after reading this short and simple book, you feel it will help other people, please help them by forwarding them a copy. Or, have them visit: **www.BigMoneySpeaker.com** and **www. MillionaireSpeakerSecrets.com**

I truly believe that, together, we can make a difference!

# PART TWO

*The 10 Mistakes
to Avoid When
Adding Public
Speaking to Your
Current Business!*

CHAPTER 2

# *Mistake #1*

## "LETTING OTHERS CONVINCE YOU THAT YOU MUST BE A GREAT SPEAKER IN ORDER TO MAKE BIG MONEY AS A SPEAKER!"

I'm about to make a statement that will make a HUGE difference in your speaking career and I'm probably one of the few people who teaches speakers who will ever tell you this.

Ready?

*"You don't have to be a great speaker in order to make a ton of money speaking!"*

That probably goes against anything you've been told by others and against what various speaker associations promote.

One of the BEST pieces of speaking advice I have ever heard in my life was stated by Lou Holtz, former Head

Football Coach at the University of Notre Dame and the University of South Carolina.

Coach Holtz gives several motivational talks a year for high fees.

Several years ago, I heard a tape of him speaking to a few thousand professional speakers at the National Convention for the National Speakers Association (NSA).

During his presentation, Coach Holtz made a comment that INSTANTLY changed my entire perception of speaking.

Coach Holtz said,

*"All speaking is, is you have something to say that helps people, then you get up on stage and say it to help them!"*

That one simple statement, changed my life.

Why? Because it just made so much sense.

I use to worry about stuff that just doesn't matter. Stuff that is nothing more than BS. Stuff that so many people in the speaking industry are telling you, like:

Worry about…

- how you walk when you're on stage
- where your hands are
- looking at each audience member

- if your clothes are too dark
- if your clothes are too light
- not flubbing your words
- using the right hand gestures
- the list goes on and on!

Prior to hearing Coach Holtz make that statement, I would be so worried about the above list and trying not to screw up, that I would actually forget what I was supposed to say in my presentation.

I'm serious!

I would stress myself out so much by worrying about all of that stuff, that I literally would be on stage and not be able to remember what to say.

Then, because of that, I began doubting whether or not I could actually succeed as a speaker, which just caused me to stress even more.

I'm so thankful that Coach Holtz made that statement because it changed my self-limiting belief. Instantly, I began believing that

I COULD succeed as a speaker.

So, now I want you to do the same.

STOP worrying about all of that stuff above and do the following:

*"Speak from your heart and just get up on stage and say things to help people!"*

See, one limiting belief that holds a lot of speakers back from making a ton of money is the belief that you need to have great speaking skills in order to make big money.

That's 100% incorrect in my book!

If that limiting belief is holding YOU back, then hopefully I can shift that belief with the following advice.

You need to get out there and share your message with others because I truly believe there's at least one person sitting in every audience who needs to hear what YOU have to say.

And, there will be times when you may think you just gave the worse presentation in the history of presentations. But I will guarantee YOU there's at least one person in every audience who needs to hear your message that day… someone who will be touched and inspired by something that comes out of your mouth during your presentation.

And, I believe you're doing <u>that</u> person a disservice by not getting out there and sharing your gifts…sharing your knowledge, tips, experience, failures, successes, strategies, and ideas that can help them.

When you think about speaking in that manner, you'll never again listen to others who try to convince you that you must be a great speaker in order to make a difference and to be able to make big money as a speaker.

*"James, thanks for all of your help with my speaking career! You're a true friend!"*

-MARK MOSELEY

**Former All-Pro & Super Bowl Champion Kicker & NFL M.V.P.**

**(Washington Redskins)**

# CHAPTER 3

# *Mistake #2*

## "LISTENING TO BS"

Y ou know what I mean when I say "Listening to BS" because I'm sure someone who tries teaching speakers has probably told you the following:

*"Dream big and you'll be on your way to having a great speaking career!"*

What a bunch of BS! You can't listen to whoever is telling you this, especially if you're paying them your hard earned dollars to "coach" you!

Here's why that whole thing about "dream big and you'll be on your way to having a great speaking career" is such a bunch of BS!

You can "dream big" as much as you want, but that doesn't get your mortgage paid…or your electric bill paid… or your heating bill paid…or your "whatever" bill paid!

Bottom line, there's only one thing that really matters in the speaking business...and don't you EVER forget it or take your eye off of it...

*"Tell me how to find the people who have the money to pay me to speak or I'm BROKE!"*

PERIOD!...That's it!...Ball game over!

I can "dream big" all I want, but if I'm not getting booked by the people in my market (or niche) that have the money to book speakers then I'm broke!

Don't you EVER forget that and don't you EVER take your eye off of that!

I wish someone taught me that years ago when I got into the speaking industry...nobody ever told me that! I was told stuff like "speak with passion" and "tell your story."

Now, don't get me wrong. I'm all about "speaking with passion" and "telling my story." But what everyone who tells you that fails to realize is that you will NEVER even have the chance to "speak with passion" or to "tell your story" if you don't FIRST get booked on the program!

See, I can be the best speaker in the world (which I'm certainly not...I'm simply decent)...I can be the best speaker in the world, but if you simply know how to find the people who have the money to pay you to speak...

and I don't...it doesn't matter how good of a speaker I am because you'll get booked over me!

But, hey...at least I'll be sitting at home "dreaming big," right!?!?!

If you decided to stop reading, right now, and if all you did from this moment forward, was to focus on implementing this one tip, I truly believe you would triple your income!

I should know because that's exactly what happened to my speaking income when I finally figured out this was:

The "KEY" that opened the treasure chest to a speaking fortune!

# CHAPTER 4

# *Mistake #3*

## "LISTENING TO SO CALLED SPEAKER COACHES WHO AREN'T CURRENTLY SPEAKING AND MAKING A TON OF MONEY AT WHAT THEY'RE CLAIMING THEY CAN TEACH YOU"

S everal years ago, I attended a function in Burbank, CA for speakers, authors, trainers, coaches and consultants. There were approximately 200 of us who were all there to hear three guest speakers talk about ways to generate more publicity.

After the three speakers gave their presentations, they sat together on stage to answer questions. I immediately raised my hand for permission to approach the crowd microphone so

I could ask my question.

After I was called on, I walked to the microphone, stated my name, the fact that I was a speaker and proceeded to ask my question. The three guest speakers were most gracious and answered my question in great detail.

As the function came to an end, I headed toward the exit when I was approached by a woman who asked if I was the "young" speaker who had asked the question. When I told her I was, she proceeded to start a conversation with me, which is listed below:

WOMAN: "James, I can take you to the next level and teach you how to earn a lot of money as a speaker."

ME: "Oh, really!?! May I ask what you do?"

WOMAN: "I'm a *Speaker Coach.*"

ME: "Do you do this for free?"

WOMAN: "No, but I'm very cheap for a *Speaker Coach.*"

ME: "How much do you charge?"

WOMAN: "I'm only $600 a month for 12 months." (which is $7,200 a year)

*NOTE* At this point, I decided to test her because I'm quite sure she had no idea that I already delivered over

1,000 highly paid talks at the time of this conversation.

ME: "Before I sign on with you for a year, may I ask you a few simple questions?"

WOMAN: "Sure," she replied as she was salivating with the thought of getting $7,200 out of me!

ME: "How many high fee paid talks did you deliver last year?"

WOMAN: "Oh…umm…I don't speak. I just *coach*."

ME: "Okay, how many high fee paid talks have you delivered in the past five or ten years?"

WOMAN: "Oh…umm…I haven't done many talks. But I have all kinds of statistical data, graphs, charts, and"…(I interrupted her)

ME: "With all do respect, I delivered over 140 high fee paid talks last year and have delivered over 1,000 talks in the past six years for high fees. What can you possibly teach me about this industry that I know like the back of my hand if you don't even speak?"

This lady was speechless with a look of horror because, basically, I just called her "bluff." I've never seen someone scurry away without saying a word faster than she did.

Be VERY careful of so called, "speaker coaches." Most of them have never been successful at getting booked and paid to speak. Yet, they'll try to dazzle you with statistical data, fancy charts, eloquent words, and persuasive sales lines.

Bottom line.....personally, I would NEVER give my hard earned money to someone who isn't extremely successful at what they're claiming they can teach me.

There's a big difference between theory and actual, hands-on, real world, battling-in-the-trenches experience.

Remember, actions speak louder than words and if they haven't done (or even better, if they aren't currently doing NOW) what they're telling you they can teach you, yet, they're trying to convince you to pay them money, then I have only one word for you.

And, you'd better perk your ears up and hear this loud and clear.

Here's my one word suggestion for you: RUN!

Actually, let me change that to a two-word suggestion:

RUN FAST!

I'm as serious as a heart attack!

Get as far away from these people as you possibly can because they will do nothing more than suck your hard-earned money out of your pockets without putting any money IN your pockets!

I wish someone taught me that back in the beginning of my career when I was listening to these so-called "speaker coaches!"

Looking back, I now realize that choosing to listen to these people was one of the main reasons my career was in a constant downward spiral!

...and, one of the main reasons I was constantly "spinning my wheels," feeling like a complete failure, ready to give-up and quit.

That leads me into the next mistake...

CHAPTER 5

# Mistake #4

"LISTENING TO PEOPLE WHO
AREN'T GETTING BOOKED,
AND MAKING BIG MONEY,
TODAY... RIGHT NOW!"

Be careful of listening to that old line that's been floating around for years. I'm sure you've heard it many times:

*"Learn from people who have been there, done that!"*

That seems fine on the surface, but it's just no good when it comes to your speaking business. I highly recommend you take it deeper than that and use *my* criteria for determining who I personally choose to learn from.

Here it is…

*"Learn from people who have been there, done that AND WHO ARE STILL DOING IT TODAY!"*

41

Just because someone has "been there, done that" doesn't mean *squat* if they still aren't out there, NOW, competing against, and getting booked over, other speakers for dates.

What happened 5, 10, or even 20 years ago, isn't relevant TODAY because the speaking industry is constantly changing.

And, there's NOBODY better to learn from than someone who's out there <u>RIGHT</u> <u>NOW</u> battling-in-the-trenches booking engagements.

Anyone trying to persuade you to believe differently, is doing nothing more than trying to be a "slick salesperson" and trying to "sell" you into paying them.

I know it's hard to believe, but there are so-called "speaker trainers" who haven't been booked for a paid talk in years, still trying to convince you they can "take you to the next level"…or, they can "make you a millionaire"…or, they can (you get the picture)!

All they're doing is "selling you on the pie-in-the-sky" and, personally, I think they're full of CRAP!

Be careful because they're really good at sounding convincing!

Here are the guidelines you need to follow…

*You need to connect with someone who, RIGHT NOW,*
*is booked more than you, at higher fees than you, in*

*markets that you want to speak in, who's not a celebrity
...and, here's the BIG deciding factor... who's making
A LOT MORE MONEY than you!*

Pursue this person and learn from them.

However, show enough respect to pay them for their knowledge, time, experience and expertise.

Don't try getting free advice. This person has no obligation, whatsoever, to share their wisdom with you.

I see so many speakers who think that just because they belong to the same speaker association, or just because they have a mutual friend, or...(you get the picture)...they're "entitled to" or "owed" the advice.

That's BS!

If you wanted sound advice from a lawyer or CPA, you would pay a fee for their advice because of their years of education, knowledge and experience.

How is it any different for getting sound advice from someone successful in the speaking industry?

And please don't use those "6 Sneaky Lines" that so many people use to try and persuade someone into helping them for FREE...

*(1) "Let's chat. I think there's some synergy between us."*

Anytime you hear the word synergy it simply means, "Hey, I'd like for you to help me!" Watch out for the synergy angle as a lot people try using it as a smooth way of getting you to help them for free.

*(2) "I just wanted to call because I feel like we're suppose to (or we should) know Each other."*

Yah, right! Why aren't they honest and say what they really mean, which is…"I'd like to know you because I think you can help me or open doors for me!"

*(3) "I just wanted to connect with you because we're both doing some great things!"*

Ho, hum! This is simply code for…"You're successful and I'd like to get information out of you!"

*(4) "I wanted to connected with you because many people have been telling me that you're really making an impact."*

Again, this is code for…"You're successful and I'd like to get information out of you!"

*(5) "I'd like to talk with you (or take you to lunch) because I'd like to PICK YOUR BRAIN!"*

What they're really trying to say is…"Let me ask you a bunch of questions but I don't want to pay you for your time because I'm too damn cheap!"

I fell for this earlier in my speaking career and met with this guy who invited me to lunch. I spent three hours with him really trying to help him. When the bill arrived he came up with some excuse about how he "forgot" his wallet and he stuck me with the bill.

I paid for the meal and never even received a thank you note in the mail for helping him or for paying the bill. As a matter of fact, he didn't even have the common courtesy to thank me while we were leaving the restaurant. He simply said that we should get together again sometime. Needless-to-say, that was the last time I ever helped him.

*(6) "I'd like you to help me because we have something in common (or because we know the same person)."*

One guy, who I never previously met, actually had the nerve to call me up one day and tell me… and I quote…

*"James, I'm thinking of getting into the speaking profession and you should help me build my speaking career because I live in the*

*state of Pennsylvania and I heard that you grew up here!"*

I'm not joking!

I never met this guy in my entire life and he actually had the nerve to tell me this.

So, my suggestion to you, if you want to work with someone, is this:

*Learn from people who have been there, done that AND WHO ARE STILL DOING IT TODAY.*

*But, show enough respect by paying for their time, knowledge, experience and expertise.*

And, prove that you're serious about learning by paying them a consulting fee...or joining their coaching/mentoring program...or, enrolling in their Boot Camp...or, (you get the picture)!

By the way, I believe the more you follow this suggestion, the more that person will bend-over backwards to help you!

# CHAPTER 6

# *Mistake #5*

## "NOT UNDERSTANDING THE #1 MARKETING MISTAKE IN BUSINESS...ESPECIALLY IN YOUR SPEAKING BUSINESS!"

I often hear speakers say,

*"I'm going to speak on 'X' topic because I really enjoy that topic."*

That is a HUGE mistake! Let me explain by sharing a simple marketing lesson.

The number one marketing mistake in any business is to, first produce a product or create a service, then try to find buyers.

Smart marketers (and speakers) look to see what the market is buying (or booking) BEFORE creating products/services (in your case which speaking topics the market is booking).

Then, they package and title their speaking topics to match exactly what the market is buying (booking).

Then, they market, market and market those speaking topics like crazy to the buyers.

If the buyers already buy (book) certain products/ services (speaking topics), then doesn't it make sense to offer the buyers what THEY WANT to buy (book), NOT what you think they want to buy (book)?

## *BIG MARKETING LESSON:*

*Give buyers what they want,*
*NOT what you think they need!*

Don't think that just because YOU love your topic and title, those who have the money to book speakers will, too! It doesn't matter what you think they need, it ONLY matters what they WANT to book!

(This one marketing lesson will revolutionize your entire career and make you a TON of money if you're not too stubborn to implement it!)

## *THE KEY:*

Research your speaking niche to determine which topics event coordinators are actually booking. Then, craft your message, and most importantly, package your speech titles and descriptions, to match <u>exactly</u> what they're looking for (booking) in topics.

I promise you'll see an immediate increase in your bookings!

Let me share a story...

In one of my recent speaker Boot Camps, a speaker named Jerry, was so determined to speak on the topic of creativity for the corporate market.

When he said that in the Boot Camp, I told him that was fine, but he would never be booked.

He said, "James, you don't understand. I see all of these books in bookstores coming out on creativity."

I said, "Jerry, you don't understand. You're talking about apples while I'm talking about oranges. I don't care what topics you see in bookstores. I read the professional speaking industry reports and I'm telling you that, for the corporate market, the following is what gets booked most:

- 80% = success, motivation, peak performance, overcoming adversity, leadership
- Then comes change, technology, customer service and sales.

So, Jerry, creativity isn't even in the top 95% of what they are booking."

I could see that Jerry became a bit discouraged when he realized this.

So, I then said,

*"But Jerry, watch this. If we simply take your topic of creativity and, rather than packaging it as a creativity talk, we simply repackage it as a talk called, 'How to Be a More Creative LEADER,' that automatically puts you in the top 80% and your topic is now something that is attractive to event coordinators."*

All of a sudden I could see Jerry grinning with enthusiasm when he realized how simple (and important) it was to repackage his talk.

Please, please, please…

STOP wasting your time and money trying to promote and market what you think event coordinators NEED to book.

And,

STOP wasting your time and money trying to get event coordinators to book what "you like to speak on."

None of that matters. The ONLY thing that matters when it comes to getting booked is,

*"Do you have a description, title and topic that event coordinators WANT to book?"*

The ONLY way you can know for sure is to RESEARCH your niche to learn EXACTLY what it is they WANT to book!

Then, package your topic, title and description to match EXACTLY what they WANT!

If you do this, have fun watching your bookings soar!

# CHAPTER 7

# Mistake #6

## "NOT RUNNING THIS AS A BUSINESS!"

Did you know that according to small business statistics, most small businesses are out of business within the 12-18 months of starting?

You may be wondering, "So what does this have to do with me?"

It's quite simple.

You need to understand one VERY important fact about being a speaker, which is:

*"You are running a BUSINESS!"*

That's right!...a business! And every business is in business to do what? That's right!...generate revenue... make a profit.

So then wouldn't it make sense to focus on trying to:

*"Extract as much revenue from every transaction?"*

The answer is YES!

See, there's so much more to this game than simply speak and get paid. That's thinking like a speaker. I want you to change how you view yourself.

Don't think like a speaker! Think like a <u>MARKETER!</u> If you do, then I guarantee you will make A LOT more money.

My way of thinking about speaking engagements is:

*"Get booked, then look for ways to make as much money as possible from EVERY booking!"*

And, that's how you need to be thinking, too!

*"Okay James, you got me. I'm into what you're saying, but what are some ways to make as much money as possible from every booking!"*

I'm glad you asked!

When I'm teaching speakers in my special live 4-day Speaker Boot Camp (for more details, **www. BigMoneySpeaker.com** and **www.MillionaireSpeaker Secrets.com**) we spend the majority of the time on this very topic.

Why? Because, I want YOU to capture all of the extra money that YOU don't even realize you're leaving on the table.

Since you are TAKING ACTION by reading this book (and have read this far) I'd like to help you by sharing this one POWERFUL idea that you should IMMEDIATELY implement!

Did you catch that?

IMMEDIATELY!

Don't just read about this idea, get off your butt and use it IMEDIATELY because it will bring you a TON of extra bookings and money, right away!

Here you go...

This "Big Money Idea" is what I call...

*"The Malinchak Referral Contract Clause"*

Why did I name it this? Because, it came to me out of thin air one evening in the very beginning of my speaking career when I was reading a contract.

When it came to me, I IMMEDIATELY added it to my speaking contract.

Did you catch that?

IMMEDIATELY!

I didn't procrastinate and think about it. I got off my butt and took action!

And, let me tell you something, it has gotten me more talks than you can imagine that have resulted in bringing me hundreds of thousands of dollars.

...and, I have used it ever since to this very day and have taught numerous speakers in my Boot Camps to use it...and they, too, have booked an astonishing number of talks and made hundreds of thousands of dollars using it.

...and, I believe YOU will book more talks than you can imagine and YOU will make more money than ever before if YOU get off your butt and TAKE ACTION by IMMEDIATELY using it.

"The Malinchak Referral Contract Clause" is simply a clause you add to your speaking contract that contractually binds the person booking you to have to refer other potential bookings to you.

Ahhh, bet you never thought about doing something like this!

And, the clause even has a line in it that contractually binds event coordinators to provide you with typed testimonial letters after your presentations. This clause will not only bring you a ton of referrals but it will also eliminate you having to continuously hound event coordinators for testimonial letters after the events.

In my actual live Speaker Boot Camps (**www. BigMoneySpeaker.com** and **www.MillionaireSpeaker Secrets.com**) I give all participants a big binder with a ton of pre-written documents that you can literally copy word-for-word. (All of the work is done for you...just use my stuff and copy it!)

How easy is that?!?!?!

I really admire and respect you for TAKING ACTION to read this book, so I've decided give you a FREE, unexpected BONUS!

Here's the actual clause that I use in my speaking contract and that I teach all the speakers who attend my live Speaker Boot Camps to use.

You may copy it word-for-word and use it in your current speaking contract:

> *If program is satisfactory, the event coordinator agrees to provide speaker with the names and contact information of two associates whose groups may benefit from booking speaker and agrees to provide a typed testimonial letter on group, organization or company letterhead stating a few positive comments about the presentation within 14 days after the event.*

Can you say cha-ching!

Now, don't just sit there. Do something with it...add it to your existing speaking contract IMMEDIATELY!

# CHAPTER 8

# *Mistake #7*

## "NOT PRE-SELLING BOOKS TO ANYONE AND EVERYONE WHO BOOKS YOU TO SPEAK!"

Recently, I mailed 74 letters and brochures to student conference coordinators and received 4 paid speaking engagements. Not bad for only a total cost of about $44.50. It's easy to do when know what to mail, who to mail it to and when to mail it.

(By the way, if you have already registered for my "Speaking Success Boot Camp" held twice a year don't worry! All of this will be covered in depth at the Boot Camp and you'll learn exactly how you can immediately begin using this strategy)

www.BigMoneySpeaker.com

www.MillionaireSpeakerSecrets.com

Getting booked to speak at these four conferences was nice, but that's not even the best part.

Early in my public speaking career, one of the conferences I was booked to speak at only had a budget of $2,500 for a keynote speaker. When I learned there would be 3,000 students and 400 advisors I immediately accepted their budgeted fee because I knew of the potential.

Most speakers would simply accept the speaking fee, sign the contract then move on. HUGE MISTAKE!!!

Remember, YOU are running a business and why are you in business? That's right, to make a profit.

Smart business-people try to make as much profit as possible from every transaction. The same should be true for YOU as a speaker.....YOU should be trying to make as much profit as possible from EVERY speaking engagement.

Let me explain exactly what I did to illustrate how I turned that $2,500 into about $33,000! Pay close attention because I want you to begin thinking this way, and if you do, I guarantee you'll begin making a tremendous amount of extra money, rather than just relying on getting your speaking fee.

I asked the event coordinator if he would be interested in having each student receive an autographed copy of one of my books, but it wouldn't cost him anything?

Naturally he said yes!

I then asked how much the registration fee was for the students to attend the conference? He said he would be setting the fee probably at $89, but it could go as high as $99. I said that if he would set the fee at $95, then each student could get a copy of my book (3,000 total students) and it wouldn't cost him anything.

He would keep $89 for conference fees while the remaining $6 would go to me to cover book printing, shipping and handling and a "small" payment to me.

In addition, I told him that we could set up a booth at the event so each student could get his/her book personally autographed.

He could even promote in his conference promotional materials that each student who attends will receive an autographed copy of my book (which retails for $11.95).

He loved the idea and said yes to the deal!

Let me share some financials with you:

- Cost to print each book: approx. $1.00 per book (Total $3,000)
- Shipping each book: approx. $.46 per book ($1,400 for 3,000)
- Total Revenue: $18,000

- Total Cost: $ 4,400
- My Book PROFIT: $13,600

## *NOTE:*

You MUST have a book to do this type of deal. Conference Coordinators WILL NOT do this for shirts, hats, posters, flyers, CDs, etc. A book is "perceived" to be of more quality. I learned this the hard way. Once I created a book, deals like this began happening.

## *ACTION STEP 1:*

Get your book finished. If you've ever hired me for consultations, then you've heard me say this to you NUMEROUS times! You can't make money like this until your book is actually done!

Make it a priority to get it done!

## *ACTION STEP 2:*

Start "thinking outside the box" when you are booked to speak! Suggest this exact type of deal. Will it happen each time? No! But what if it did happen only one time? Would you have a problem accepting the extra money? Didn't think so! By the way, this is the THIRD deal I've done THIS YEAR and I'm currently working on another right now! Do the math on the extra money!

Here's the rest of the story of how I took the $16,100 ($2,500 Speaking Fee + $13,600 Book Profit) to $33,000:

Since I would be speaking at 8:30 p.m. on a Friday night at the conference, I mailed my speaking brochure to all the college coordinators within a 3-hour drive of where I'll be speaking asking if they would be interested in a "block-booking" for their campus at a reduced rate since I'll be in their area. I emphasized there wouldn't be any expenses since I would already be in their area.

Out of the 34 colleges 4 said yes (12% return......not bad). My normal college rate is $4,000-$8,500, but I offered them a block-booking rate of $2,500 flat (meaning no expenses).

- 4 Colleges x $2,500       =       $10,000

I then mailed to about 20 high schools in the area with the same block-booking offer, only I offered them a speaking fee of $1,000 flat. Two high schools said yes (10% return)!

- 2 High Schools x $1,000     =       $2,000
- Total Additional Income     =       $28,100

PLUS, at the conference I keynoted I sold my other books and motivational cassettes/CDs. Typically, I can count on about 10% of the audience buying additional products (I know this from tracking my results from past conferences...you should be tracking all of your results too).

- 3,400 Audience Members x 10% = 340 buyers

I offered a great package deal at the conference to make sure it was too good for them to pass up. I gave them two of my other books, a cassette of my live talk and a CD of my live talk for $20. Why $20? Because when people go to conferences they typically carry $20 bills in their wallets.

- My total cost for each package = $5
- ($1 per product plus shipping them to the conference)
- My total profit per package = $15
- 340 Buyers x $15 = $5,100 EXTRA PROFIT!

### *TOTAL INCOME:*

| | | |
|---|---|---|
| • Speaking Fee: | $ | 2,500 |
| • Book Deal: | $ | 13,600 |
| • College Talks: | $ | 10,000 |
| • High School Talks: | $ | 2,000 |
| • Product Sales: | $ | 5,100 |
| **TOTAL:** | **$33,200** | |

Can you say Cha Ching!

YOU should be following the exact process I just described above!

By the way, I'll be teaching exactly how to do all this stuff and MORE at the "Speaking Success Boot Camp." If you've previously called or emailed me about your interest in attending, but you're still sitting on your butt procrastinating, then what are you waiting for?

Get off your butt and take action!

Your bookings and income WILL NOT change until you make the decision!

**www.BigMoneySpeaker.com**

**www.MillionaireSpeakerSecrets.com**

CHAPTER 9

# Mistake #8

## "MODELING YOUR CAREER AFTER A FAMOUS SPEAKER!"

I am so tired of hearing speakers say, "I'm going to become famous"…or, "I'm going to be the next Tony Robbins"…or, "I'm going to be the next Les Brown"…or, "I'm going to be the next (whoever)!"

Why in the world would you want to be the next anybody!?!

Be the first, and only, YOU!

Create your own uniqueness, your own style, your own methods, your own following.

I'm not saying that you shouldn't observe famous speakers. I believe you can always learn a few things from observing anyone.

Fellow speaker, Larry Winget, makes a great point that relates perfectly. Larry says,

*"Don't do what they do, just do it the way they do it!"*

I believe that trying to model your career after a famous speaker is a HUGE mistake.

Here's why…

You and I are not like most famous speakers. They caught a big break somewhere along the line that either…

- put them on television
- had a movie made about their life
- created a best-selling book series
- won a Gold medal in the Olympics
- came in first place on reality television show
- played in the Super Bowl
  …the list goes on and on

I'm not saying that one (or more) of those things couldn't happen for you. And if any did happen, then I'd be very happy for you and the first one to congratulate you.

However, the chance of one of those things happening for you or I are not likely. Plus, one of those things rarely happens overnight and without months, even years, of hard work.

Even if you were fortunate enough to win first place on a reality television show or write, promote and sell a best-selling book (which seems about the quickest of those listed above), it still would require and enormous amount of time, energy, effort and hard work.

I see so many talented speakers "spinning their wheels" by spending so much time on trying to create the "big break," they lose out on hundreds of thousands of dollars that speakers like me, and those I've taught, gobble up.

<u>It's not really their fault because that's what so many people in the speaking industry program them to believe they need to do in order to make big money as a speaker.</u>

Could becoming famous help them?

Of course it could.

But it's not necessary!

And, I'm living proof of that because I'm NOT famous, yet, I make a ton of money each and every year!

What I prefer to do is model my career after non-celebrity speakers who are making a TON of money because they're obviously doing something right.

My personal focus is one thing:

*"Get Booked!"*

That's it! Period!

You may have never heard of me prior to subscribing to my "Big Money Speaker Tips" ezine at:

www.BigMoneySpeaker.com
www.MillionaireSpeakerSecrets.com

However, it doesn't matter because thousands of event coordinators who have the money to book me to speak have heard of me.

And, that's all that matters in this speaking game!

So here's a BIG marketing lesson you REALLY need to grasp:

*"Just Because YOU Haven't Heard of a Particular Speaker in a Market, Don't Assume He/She Isn't Successful & Making a Ton of Money!"*

One thing I've consistently done for the past nine years, is study and learn from the world's top <u>MARKETERS.</u>

Why?

Because that's what my wealthy, successful cousin suggested back when my career was going down the drain.

I've been studying, learning from and hanging out with people you've probably never heard of like...

Dan Kennedy who, other than Zig Ziglar, is the only speaker to appear in all of the big Peter Lowe Success Rallies where the average audience is about 15,000. Sure the rallies have speakers like George Bush, Larry King and several other celebrities who get paid $20,000-$100,000 a talk. But Dan makes more than all of them.

In addition to Dan's speaking fee, he makes anywhere from $70,000-$150,000 in product sales at EACH EVENT...no this is not a misprint...EACH EVENT! And, he does about 20 of these types of events a year. Do the math and see how much he makes just from 20 events.

I'm telling you about Dan because there's an important marketing lesson here which is....just because you may have never heard of a certain speaker, don't assume he/she isn't speaking a lot and making a lot of money.

Let me share a personal example...

You probably know by now that one of the markets I've talked in...and made a lot of money in...for the past 9 years has been the college market.

And, you know that because of all the requests I was getting from speakers to help them get started in this market, I finally gave in and agreed to put in the enormous amount of time and effort to put on a weekend Boot Camp in Las Vegas teaching speakers how to make serious money in the college market.

There are two reasons I offer the Boot Camp. One, is that I love helping other speakers and teaching them how to add hundreds of thousands of dollars to their income. I really don't think it's difficult to instantly double or triple your speaking income if you will simply implement the savvy marketing strategies that I teach.

The second reason for offering the Boot Camp is to weed out those who are the lookers from those who are the doers.

I'm more than happy to help anyone who is serious, but tired of wasting my time with those who aren't serious. Those who attend the Boot Camp know that I bust my butt to help them and make it my personal mission to teach them all the marketing secrets

I use that can make them a ton of money. And, I'm passionate about it!

Those who don't attend, I've decided, I'm not wasting my time with anymore.

Why?

Because it says to me that someone who isn't willing to "invest in themselves" to attend and learn everything they need to know in one measly 4-day Boot Camp, isn't serious about reaching the next level.

We've received several calls and emails from speakers who knew of me and want to register. But we also received calls and emails from speakers who didn't know of me and had questions.

One speaker called and wanted to talk with me so he could basically question me to see if I really knew what I was talking about. He said he's been speaking on the college circuit for years and has only heard of me a little.

He began by asking that if I knew so much about the college speaking market then why hasn't he seen me standing at a conference exhibit booth that a major student activities association puts on every year?

My response was,

*"Why would I want to try to get bookings in the exact place that thousands of other speakers, comedians, hypnotists, magicians, bands, speakers bureaus, agencies and who knows who else goes to market? That's one of the worse marketing moves I've ever heard!"*

I told him that I wasn't implying that being a member of that particular association was a bad move, just not the smartest.

I then told him that I'm a member of the association (primarily to get the mailing list of the coordinators). However, when it comes to getting booked, I find all the organizations who could book me to speak at colleges and student conferences that <u>other speakers don't know about.</u>

Then I began naming 2 or 3 (out of the 10-15 that I market to) while also sharing a few strategies I use to get booked over other speakers he HAS heard of on the college circuit.

To make a long story short, after about an hour on the phone with this guy, I had his head spinning with so many new ideas for how he could instantly get bookings.

After speaking with him for this hour and sharing these ideas, he apologized numerous times for assuming that I didn't know what I was talking about simply because HE hadn't really heard of me even though he had been in that market for years.

By the way, he immediately signed up for the Boot Camp because he quickly realized that if he wanted to make the kind of serious money that I (and those who I've taught) make, then he needed to get off his butt and "invest in himself."

The reason I told you that personal story is so you hopefully caught the underlying message that I've been trying to drive home to you:

*"Just Because YOU Haven't Heard of a Particular Speaker in a Market, Don't Assume He/She Isn't Successful & Making a Ton of Money!"*

So, back to Mistake #8: Modeling Your Career After a Famous Speaker

Don't fall into the trap that I see so many talented speakers fall into by trying to model your speaking career after a famous speaker.

If you are currently in that trap right now, STOP!

You are <u>wasting</u> so much valuable time, energy, effort and money trying to become *famous* that YOU are losing out on speaking engagements to speakers like me who don't focus on the "famous thing."

And, YOU are missing out on hundreds of thousands of dollars in extra money YOU could be putting in your pockets!

Here's one of my personal philosophies that I follow for my own speaking business and I'm going to encourage you to follow it, as well.

*"Don't fill your ego, fill your bank account!"*

You should adopt it, follow it and keep reminding yourself of this daily. Why? Because it's so easy to get caught up in the whole,

*"I've got to get on the* Oprah *television show"*

*...or,*

*"I've got to get in the* USA Today *newspaper"*

*...or,*

*"I've got to write the next* Chicken Soup for the Soul *book series"*

*or,*

*"I've got to do (fill in the blank) to become famous!"*

*I'm living proof that YOU don't need to be*
*a famous speaker to make BIG money.*

So, stop wasting your money and time on trying to become a famous speaker. If it happens for you as you're making a ton of money, then great. If not, so what! <u>At least you still have a ton of money in your bank account!</u>

Give me the choice between "being famous" or "making a ton of money, each and every year" and I'll take the money <u>EVERY</u> time!

When you walk into your bank to deposit a check from a speaking engagement, the teller will never say to you,

*"I'm sorry. We can't deposit your check for you because you're not a famous speaker."*

The bank will always accept your check, so why would you care if you're famous or not!?! That's focusing on "filling your ego!"

Again, remember: "Don't fill your ego, fill your bank account!"

From this day forward, only focus your time, energy, effort and money on the following:

> *"The KEY and the ONLY thing you should be focusing your time, energy, effort and money on is getting known by the people in the niche market you want to speak in who have the money to book YOU to speak!"*

That's it!

Find them and market to them OVER and OVER and OVER again!

And, if you do, you'll make more money as a speaker than you could ever imagine!

# CHAPTER 10

# *Mistake #9*

"NOT MAKING THE DECISION
THAT INVESTING IN
YOURSELF ON A CONTINUOUS
BASIS IS PROFOUNDLY
IMPORTANT IF YOU WANT
TO CONTINUE CLIMBING
TO HIGHER AND HIGHER
INCOME LEVELS!"

I t totally amazes me that so many speakers moan and complain about how they're tired of not making enough money, <u>yet, they refuse to do anything about it!</u>

One of my favorite quotes I heard is:

*"If you keep on doing what you've been doing then you'll keep on getting what you've been getting, so don't be surprised!"*

79

I honestly believe that all of the knowledge you need to book more talks…make a ton of money…take your business to the next level, etc., is out there.

You just need to do whatever you have to do in order to get it.

But, unless YOU decide to take a portion of your income and "invest it back in yourself" so that you can get the kind of strategies, tips, and shortcuts like I'm sharing with you in this Special Report, then YOU won't make more money!

I believe this 100%!

But, it's <u>profoundly</u> <u>important</u> to make sure you <u>ONLY</u> "invest in yourself" with those who will SAVE and MAKE you money IMMEDIATELY!

<u>Don't fall for the BS "fluff" like I did when I was "spinning my wheels" as a speaker, feeling like a complete failure, ready to give-up and quit</u>

So, back to my point, if you're stuck in a rut, right now, then,

*"Don't just there, DO something about it…NOW!"*

Decide to get off of your butt, take responsibility for yourself and for what you are or aren't getting in your speaking career. That was the first step for me getting out of my rut. I had to take responsibility for choosing to listen to the wrong people!

Make the commitment to yourself to seek out and invest in whatever CD program, DVD program, seminar, training session, workshop or Boot Camp that you need to invest in so you can quickly begin making big money.

Notice, I didn't say, "spend money on." I said, "invest in," because you MUST STOP thinking of it as though you are spending money.

That's the way a "poverty conscious speaker" thinks.

From this moment forward, I want you to "shift your thinking" and join me, and the speakers I've helped, in thinking like a:

*"Prosperity Conscious Speaker!"*

Someone who understands the importance of, believes in, and is committed to follow what Tony Robins calls CANI:

**C**onstant

**A**nd

**N**ever-Ending

**I**mprovement

But don't just invest in yourself once. If you really want to make big money from speaking, each and every year for the rest of your life, then you need to make this a consistent part of your business so it becomes a habit that you continuously practice.

Here are three more favorite quotes that I have in my office so I can see them everyday.

Why everyday?

Because, I want to continuously remind myself how <u>profoundly important</u> it is to "keep investing in myself!" It seems simple, but it's revolutionary!

*"An investment in yourself always pays the best interest!"*

-BEN FRANKLIN

*"Your personal income will seldom exceed your personal development!"*

-JIM ROHN

*"If you think investing in yourself is expensive, then you should try ignorance!"*

-UNKNOWN

Personally, I've "invested" over $100,000 the past few years in myself!

$100,000!?!

Yep!

And, let me tell you, that's a bargain considering the number of bookings and the amount of money that "investment" continues bringing back to me year after year!

I would not be where I am today...getting the number of high fee bookings that I get...meeting the people that I meet...making the kind of big money that I make...if I hadn't made the decision and commitment several years ago to "invest in myself" to get CD programs, DVD programs, attend Boot Camps, etc.

I believe that 100%!

I am where I am because of consistently practicing the habit of continuously "investing in myself."

<u>I'm nothing special.</u> I just got off my butt and "invested in myself" to learn what I needed to do in order to make big money!

That's why it totally amazes me when I hear speakers moan and complain about not making enough money, <u>yet, they don't do anything about it.</u>

One thing that is very important to note. I would never consider trying to get information for free.

I respect anyone who has put in their time, energy, effort and "investment" to learn what I'd like to know and I'm more than happy to pay them by "investing in myself" to learn from them.

Last year, alone, I did the following:

- Invested (not paid) $5,000 plus another $1,000 in expenses to sit in a guys home office for 3 days, watching how he runs his Internet business that brings him over $1,000,000 a year from working at home.

Was it worth it?

Oh yah!

Within the first two hours of sitting in his home office, he showed me how I was blowing about $2,500 per year with one little, stupid mistake that I didn't even realize I was making.

And, it only took him spending about 5-minutes on it for me to see those 5-minutes were worth the entire $5,000 I invested in the entire weekend.

Why?

Because, let's say that I now save $2,500 each year for the next 10 years. That's $2,500 I saved per year (or, you can look at it as $2,500 that I'm now making per year), multiplied by ten years, would equal a $25,000 savings over 10 years!

Let's see…hmm…

I invested $5,000 <u>ONCE</u>, but get back $2,500 a year in savings <u>EVERY</u> year for the rest of my career!

Sounds pretty sweet to me!

Plus, from all of the other strategies that he showed me, I anticipate adding an extra $100,000+ in Internet revenue to my current income each year!

Plus, he and I are doing a seminar together that should easily bring us an extra $50,000+ each!

Add all of this together and you can easily see how the initial $5,000 invested was NOTHING compared to what it will return for me in the present and for the rest of my career.

- Invested (not paid) $2,500 plus another $1,000 in expenses to attend a 4-day training to learn product platform selling from a guy who has sold as much as $350,000 after one 90-minute presentation. (No, this is not a misprint!)

Was it worth it?

Big time!

Because of changing just a few things that I say during my presentations...tips that I learned from this guy...I noticed an immediate "jump" in product sales.

I recently did $33,500 in product sales after one 90-minute presentation to an audience of only 69 people.

And,

I recently did $16,300 in product sales after one 45-minute presentation to an audience of only 52 people.

And,

I have a talk coming up for 200 people where I anticipate selling anywhere from $50,000-$70,000 in products after a 90-minute presentation.

Let's see…hmm…

I invested $2,500 <u>ONCE</u>, but already did $49,800 in product sales because of changing just a few lines in my talk that I learned from this guy.

Again, sounds pretty sweet to me!

So, let me ask you a <u>very </u>important question. And, I want you to honestly answer it. Be completely honest with yourself. It's the first step to making positive, productive, lasting change:

Are you currently thinking like a...

*"Poverty Conscious Speaker"*
*or like a,*
*"Prosperity Conscious Speaker?"*

If you're currently thinking like a "poverty conscious speaker" it's perfectly okay. Don't beat yourself up over it. You're not alone. I've done it, too, prior to shifting my mindset.

And, it's probably not even your fault because nobody has ever taught you how <u>profoundly</u> <u>important</u> it is to "shift your thinking!"

UNTIL NOW!

Here's what I want you to do, RIGHT NOW!

1) Make the decision to immediately "shift your thinking" to be a "Prosperity Conscious Speaker!"

    It's really as simple as MAKING A DECISION! Don't think it's more difficult than that. But, please don't downplay the importance of making this DECISION! The power to <u>choose</u> the path YOU want to follow in life is the most profoundly important power within you!

    I love what Tony Robbins says,

> *"It's in the moment of your decisions*
> *that your destiny is created!"*

2) Start <u>immediately</u> "investing in yourself!" Again, notice I didn't say, "spend money on yourself." Take some kind of immediate action to get any kind of information that will help take you to the next level.

There's an old saying, "Experience is the best teacher."

I don't model my speaking career after that saying.

I prefer modeling my speaking career after this:

### *"OTHER PEOPLE'S experience is the best teacher!"*

Learn from people who are playing at higher levels than you and let their knowledge, experience, tips, strategies, ideas, and shortcuts pull you up to that level.

But don't procrastinate! Start RIGHT NOW!

Remember, "Don't just there, DO something about it… NOW!"

Because, if <u>YOU</u> <u>CHOOSE</u> not to…

"Then you'll keep on doing what you've been doing and you'll keep on getting what you've been getting, so don't be surprised!"

# CHAPTER 11

# *Mistake #10*

"NOT LEARNING FROM
<u>SOMEONE</u> <u>JUST</u> <u>LIKE</u> <u>YOU</u>...
WHO UNDERSTANDS WHAT
YOU'RE GOING THROUGH...
(BECAUSE HE'S BEEN THERE)
AND WHO TRULY CARES
ABOUT HELPING YOU
MAKE BIG MONEY!"

This is one of the critical KEYS to your success as a speaker.

Why? Because there are so many people out there who care more about your money than you, your career and your vision.

Believe me, I know!

Because as I stated earlier in this Special Report, looking back, I now realize that choosing to listen to these people was one of the main reasons my career was in a constant downward spiral!

...and, one of the main reasons I was constantly "spinning my wheels," feeling like a complete failure, ready to give-up and quit.

That's the main reason why I wrote this Special Report and why I began helping speakers.

I just got SO fed up with hearing all of the BS these people have been feeding you, me and the thousands of other speakers just like us.

I just couldn't take it anymore!

I literally started getting sick to my stomach every time I heard that someone like you was being misinformed and was being led down a road that would NEVER lead you to making big money.

I'm serious. These people BS-ing you made me want to puke!

Finally, a few years ago, I just couldn't stand it anymore.

So, at the urging of a few speakers that I was helping, I decided to make it a personal mission of mine to help as many speakers as possible to make big money.

There's nothing that makes me more fulfilled and gets me more excited than when someone like you says,

*"Thank you for helping me and for changing my life!"*

I remember a very successful speaker calling me one day as he was out in a park playing with his kids to say the following:

*"James, I just wanted to call to say thank you!*

*Because of attending your Boot Camp and what you taught me, my life, my wife's life and my kid's lives will never be the same.*

*You not only taught me how to think differently and how to get big money speaking deals, but you also showed me so many ways to make big money and how easy it is to do.*

*Because of what you taught me, I'll never have to work for anyone else, again, the rest of my life!*

*I'm so thankful that Dusty (another speaker) referred me to you. I don't even want to think where my career would be had I not met you!"*

Don't get me wrong, I do like making big money, as I'm sure you can tell from the focus of this Book.

But, there's nothing that touches my heart more than when someone like you listens to what I share, implements it, then calls or emails to tell me how you've instantly booked more talks...or, sold thousands of dollars worth of products...or, made a ton of EXTRA money!

And, my fulfillment doesn't actually come from YOU making big money. It really comes from what YOU will now be able to experience as a result of adding hundreds of thousands of dollars in EXTRA income each year to your pockets!

See, I believe what my friend Mark Victor Hansen says. Mark is the Co-creator of the #1 Best-selling book series, *Chicken Soup for the Soul* and Co-author of the two recent top-sellers, *The One Minute Millionaire* and *Crackin' Millionaire Code.*

Mark says,

*"You need MONEY freedom because that gives you TIME freedom. And, when you have time freedom, you get RELATIONSHIP freedom!"*

Money is not the answer to everything. But the more money you have, the more time you can spend with your children, husband, wife, friends, family members, church, community, etc.

Also, the more money you have the LESS STRESS you will have because you won't be worrying about:

- paying your mortgage payment
- making your car payment
- paying for your children's college education
- having enough put away for retirement
- caring for aging parents
- paying for travel and vacation expenses
- helping your church, community, charities or those less fortunate
- and, so on!

I know we may not personally know each other. But I want you know that I truly care about helping you.

And, I hope that what I've shared with you in this book has helped you!

I know that most of what I've shared with you has been very direct and to-the-point. But I began this book by telling you:

*"One thing I can promise you is that I will NOT BS you and give you 'fluff!'*

*I can't stand when people in the speaking industry do that.*

*My style is direct, straight-forward, and I don't pull punches!*

*My main focus is to help you and give you 'real' ideas that will instantly SAVE, and MAKE, you a TON of money!"*

I wanted to tell you what I thought you <u>NEEDED</u> to hear!

Why? Because I wish someone would have taught me these things back when I was "spinning my wheels" as a speaker, feeling like a complete failure, ready to give-up and quit.

I knew you would be 100% better off after reading this information. Remember, I know what you're probably going through because I've been there.

<u>I understand how frustrating it can be to know that YOU have the potential to make big money, but for some unexplained reason it just doesn't happen!</u>

Don't let this bring you down, because I've been there many times in the past. Although it can be frustrating at times, here's some good news. And, I believe without a doubt this is the KEY that immediately TRIPLED my speaking income:

*"Once I decided to STOP listening to all of those people who were filling my head with BS, my career and life instantly changed!"*

And, I know your career and life will instantly change, too, when you do the same!

You don't even need to believe, right now, that you can add hundreds of thousands of dollars in EXTRA income each year!

All you have to do is believe that I KNOW YOU CAN DO IT!

*"You CAN Do it!*
*You Can Do it Here!*
*And, You CAN Do it NOW!"*

There's only one thing left for you to do: TAKE ACTION!

If I've helped you with what I've shared with you in this Special Report, then I'd love to help you even more!

Here's what I want you to do RIGHT NOW!

Contact me, and tell me how you've been helped with this information. I can be reached through my website at:

**www.BigMoneySpeaker.com**
**www.MillionaireSpeakerSecrets.com**

And, if you're <u>REALLY</u> ready to take your speaking career to a much higher level and make more money speaking than you ever dreamed possible, then make the wise decision to **"invest**

**in yourself"** to attend my next Speaker's Boot Camp or get my Home Study Courses.

**If you're serious, then I really want you to attend the live Boot Camp or, at least, get one of the Home Study Courses because I know the information will change your life and bring YOU a ton of money!**

I guarantee, this will be the **<u>BEST</u>** investment YOU ever make in your entire speaking career!

But, don't take my word for it. Re-read the testimonials from <u>speakers</u> <u>just</u> <u>like</u> <u>you</u> that I've helped. They were all cautious before attending the Boot Camp, but after they attended, they

**ALL** agreed it was the **BEST** investment in their speaking careers they **EVER** made!

And I guarantee <u>YOU WILL FEEL THE SAME</u> after you've attended!

**Let me show you how to instantly book more talks and make more money speaking than you ever dreamed possible!**

**YOU can do it, and YOU can do it NOW!**

# ABOUT THE AUTHOR

*James Malinchak* was born and raised in a small Pennsylvania steel-mill town (Monessen) and doesn't have any advanced academic degrees, hasn't won any speech contests and has never been awarded any speaker designations from any speaker associations. Yet, he is still one of the most requested speakers in America.

James is known as "The Big Money Speaker," is the Founder of the top speaker training web sites:

**www.BigMoneySpeaker.com**

**www.www.CollegeSpeakingSuccesss.com**

**www.MillionaireSpeakerSecrets.com**

James is <u>NOT</u> a speaker coach! He is someone who <u>IS</u> doing what he teaches and because of that, speakers have sought him out to learn from him. He has taught numerous people how to make big money as a public speaker through his live Boot Camps, home study courses and exclusive, private coaching programs.

James has delivered over 2,000 presentations for entrepreneur groups, corporations, businesses, colleges, universities and large youth events. He's written 16 books, recorded numerous audio programs and has shared the speaking stages with some of the biggest celebrity speakers. He's also been interviewed on the VIP Red Carpet by Celebrity Interviewer Robin Leach and was interviewed by Joan Rivers on the hit Reality TV Show, "How'd You Get So Rich?"

# BUY A SHARE OF THE FUTURE IN YOUR COMMUNITY

These certificates make great holiday, graduation and birthday gifts that can be personalized with the recipient's name. The cost of one S.H.A.R.E. or one square foot is $54.17. The personalized certificate is suitable for framing and will state the number of shares purchased and the amount of each share, as well as the recipient's name. The home that you participate in "building" will last for many years and will continue to grow in value.

**Here is a sample SHARE certificate:**

THIS CERTIFIES THAT
**YOUR NAME HERE**
HAS INVESTED IN A HOME FOR A DESERVING FAMILY
**1985-2005**
TWENTY YEARS OF BUILDING FUTURES IN OUR
COMMUNITY ONE HOME AT A TIME
1200 SQUARE FOOT HOUSE @ $65,000 = $54.17 PER SQUARE FOOT
This certificate represents a tax deductible donation. It has no cash value.

## YES, I WOULD LIKE TO HELP!

*I support the work that Habitat for Humanity does and I want to be part of the excitement! As a donor, I will receive periodic updates on your construction activities but, more importantly, I know my gift will help a family in our community realize the dream of homeownership.* **I would like to SHARE in your efforts against substandard housing in my community!** *(Please print below)*

PLEASE SEND ME _____ SHARES at $54.17 EACH = $ $_____

*In Honor Of:* _____

*Occasion: (Circle One)*    HOLIDAY    BIRTHDAY    ANNIVERSARY

      OTHER: _____

*Address of Recipient:* _____

*Gift From:* _____ *Donor Address:* _____

*Donor Email:* _____

**I AM ENCLOSING A CHECK FOR $ $_____ PAYABLE TO HABITAT FOR HUMANITY OR PLEASE CHARGE MY VISA OR MASTERCARD** *(CIRCLE ONE)*

Card Number _____ Expiration Date: _____

Name as it appears on Credit Card _____ Charge Amount $ _____

Signature _____

Billing Address _____

Telephone # Day _____ Eve _____

**PLEASE NOTE:** Your contribution is tax-deductible to the fullest extent allowed by law.
**Habitat for Humanity • P.O. Box 1443 • Newport News, VA 23601 • 757-596-5553**
**www.HelpHabitatforHumanity.org**

LaVergne, TN USA
22 October 2009
161747LV00001B/5/P